LONDON

DISTRIBUTOR: FISA (GREAT BRITAIN) Ltd. - 22 B, Wolsey Road LONDON N. 1 - Telephone: 020 7254 0976

Editorial Escudo de Oro, S.A.

One of the earliest paintings of
London, circa *1500.*

King John's Charter, *1215.*

The Great Fire of London, *1666.*

The Monument. Built in 1677 to commemorate the great fire of London.

THE CITY

Modern London is a hybrid creature formed from the ancient cities of London and Westminster evolving over the centuries into what is today a sprawling metropolis comprising some 8,000,000 inhabitants in an area of about 610 square miles. But it is in the City that we must look for the origins of the London we know today. London, the greatest city in the world, is at least two thousand years old and was settled long before the first Roman invansion. Over the centuries the City has jealously guarded its independence which has been recognised by a series of royal charters. William the Conqueror acknowledged the City's special privileges as did King John in a Charter dated 9 May 1215 which confirmed the right to choose a Mayor by annual election.

The medieval face of London was dramatically changed by the Great Fire which broke out on 2 September 1666 in Pudding Lane, less than a year after the Great Plague that in a single week had claimed over 12,000 lives. During a period of four days 13,000 houses and over 80 churches were destroyed. The Great Fire consumed many of the fine livery halls of the City Companies, the Royal Exchange, the Guildhall (only the walls and crypt escaped) the Fish Market at Billingsgate, Fleet and Bridewell Prisons, Ludgate, Aldersgate and Newgate (three of the ancient City gates), and St. Paul's Cathedral. Miraculously only a few lives were lost but the Fire destroyed over three-quarters of the City and along with it priceless records and fine examples of medieval architecture both civil and religious. *The Monument* was designed by Sir Christopher Wren, in collaboration with Robert Hooke, and erected in 1677 to commemorate the Great Fire. The Portland stone fluted column is 202 feet high, surmounted by a platform and topped by a gilded flaming urn. The height is reputed to be the exact distance from where the fire started. Three hundred and eleven steps inside the pillar lead to a balcony from which there is a marvellous view of London. "The Fat Boy", a small gilded wooden figure situated high up on a wall in Cock Lane, Giltspur Street, Smithfield, marks the farthest limit of the Fire.

The Central Criminal Court, more popularly known as the Old Bailey, was built in 1907 near the site of the infamous Newgate which was London's main prison from the thirteenth century. Contrary to popular belief the figure of Justice, topping the copper dome, holding a sword in one hand and the scales of justice in the other, is *not* blindfolded.

Doctor Johnson's House, Gough Square, off Fleet Street is a delightful example of Queen Anne domestic architecture. The Doctor lived here between 1748-1759 and compiled his famous *Dictionary* in the attic at the top of the house with the help of six assistants. The house contains many Johnson relics including his armchair, letters and prints of friends — Mrs. Thrale, Fanny Burney, Oliver Goldsmith, David Garrick, Sir Joshua Reynolds and his biographer

Temple Bar (left), The Guildhall (bottom), and (top) The Fat Boy.

James Boswell. The nearby *Cheshire Cheese* in Wine Court Lodge was a popular eating-place for Johnson and his contemporaries as it is today for the tourist. Johnson might well have been thinking of this seventeenth-century tavern when he said "There is nothing which has yet been contrived by man, by which so much happiness is produced as by a good tavern or inn".

Within this one square mile of concentrated history and amid the continuously changing face of the City is the world's financial and commercial centre. *Lloyd's,* typical of so many City institutions, was founded in a coffee shop at the end of the seventeenth century. Originally concerned exclusively with maritime insurance, today its syndicates of some 5,000 members underwrite an astonishing range of world-wide risks. In the centre of the Underwriting Room hangs the Lutine Bell which is rung to mark an important announcement — one stroke means bad news and two good news. The bell came from the frigate *La Lutine* which sank in 1799 a cargo of gold which was insured by Lloyd's.

The Guildhall, or the Hall of Guilds, is the seat of City government for here is where the Court of Common Council meets. The election of the Lord Mayor and Sheriffs and state banquets take place in the Great Hall with much pomp and pageantry. In this same hall the unfortunate Lady Jane Grey (the nine-day Queen) and her husband were tried and sentenced to death in 1553. The two giant carved figures at the far end of the Great Hall are Gog and Magog, modern versions of the originals which were destroyed in the Great Fire. The present building dates from the beginning of the

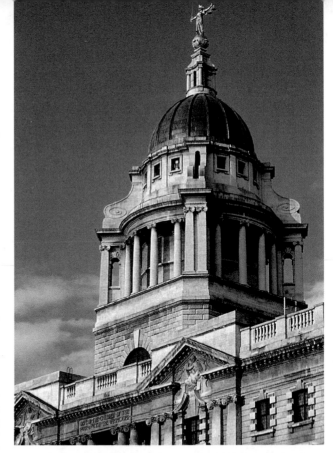

fifteenth century though it suffered much damage during the Great Fire and again in the Second World War.

The Mansion House is the official residence of the Lord Mayor of London. Behind the Corinthian portico are many sumptuous apartments, the Court of Justice with cells below, and the Egyptian Hall used for state banquets.

Since 1970 the *Stock Exchange* has been housed in a new twenty-six storeyed complex in Old Broad Street. Visitors can watch this great financial institution in action from a gallery overlooking the "floor of the house". "My word is my bond" *(Dictum Meum Pactum)* is the motto of the Stock Exchange and today even among the sophisticated computer gadgetry verbal transactions are the basic form of business.

The Bank of England was founded in 1694 largely to finance the French wars during the reign of William and Mary. Within the vaults of "the Old Lady of Threadneedle Street" are kept the nation's gold reserves. The Bank was an independent company up to 1946 when it was nationalised and control passed to the Treasury.

The Royal Exchange was first founded about 1565 by that great financier, Sir Thomas Gresham, for "merchants to assemble in", but this building was destroyed in the Great Fire of London (1666) and its successor suffered a similar fate in 1838. The present building dates from 1844 but no business has been conducted from it since 1939. The equestrian statue of the Duke of Wellington is noted for its absence of stirrups.

The Temple of Mithras. During the preparation of the site for Bucklersbury House in 1954 the Roman Temple of Mithras was revealed. Subsequent excavations proved this to be a unique discovery; a pagan temple, dedicated to the Persian Sun-god. The Temple was later reconstructed only a short way from its original site and the relics are currently displayed in the new Museum of London in the Barbican.

London Stone was rescued from the ruins of St. Swithin's Church bombed in the last War, and set in the wall of the office building which stands on the same site. This stone is thought to be a Roman milestone from which distances were measured along the whole chain of Roman roads radiating from the City all over the country.

The Barbican is an imaginative development scheme in the northern part of the City covering an area of some thirty-five acres which had been devastated during the last War. It comprises multi-storey blocks of offices and some of the highest blocks of flats in Europe, shops, taverns, restaurants, an Arts Centre and a new Museum of London. A brave attempt by the planning authorities to provide a self-contained community with residential accommodation for some 6,500 people to live near the heart of the City.

CITY
OF
LONDON

The Tower and Tower Bridge from the north-west.

THE TOWER OF LONDON

The approach to the Tower is by way of Tower Hill, the site of so many public executions in the past, but where today the public are more peacefully entertained by politicians, preachers, and "buskers".

There is more of London's history in the Tower than anywhere else. It is the oldest surviving building in London, dating from the Norman Conquest, and even before that the site had been used by the Romans, and later by the Saxons as a fortress.

From the eleventh century onwards the Tower has served many purposes — always a fortress but, at various periods of history, also as a royal palace (King Charles II was the last king to stay here and before him, King Henry III); a prison (the long list of unfortunate inmates includes Kings, Queens, Princes and Nobles); a treasury; a mint until 1810; an arsenal; the first royal observatory in the reign of King Charles II; and for three hundred years there was a royal zoo which was moved to Regent's Park in the 1830's.

The oldest part is the White Tower built as a fortress and family residence by William the Conqueror in 1078. The name is said to have originated in the reign of King Henry III who ordered the Tower to be whitewashed. Today the White Tower houses a unique collection of arms and armour and instruments of torture. The Chapel of St. John, on the first floor, is one of the finest surviving specimens of pure Norman architecture — a wonderful combination of immense strength with an impressive simplicity of line. Apart from the windows, which were enlarged by Sir Christopher Wren, the chapel is virtually in its original state. The Chapel has a long recorded history as it was within these walls that the Archbishop of Canterbury and the Chancellor were seized in 1381 during the Peasants' Revolt and taken to be murdered on Tower Hill; King Henry VI's body lay here after his murder in 1471; Mary Tudor went through a form of marriage by proxy to Philip, King of Spain; Lady Jane Grey (the nine-day Queen) prayed here before her execution in 1553. Candidates for the Order of the Bath, the second oldest Order of Knighthood, kept their

The White Tower.

Traitor's Gate.

The Salt Tower.

Elizabeth's Walk.

The Western entrance to the Tower via the Middle and Byward Towers.

Upper chamber of the Wakefield Tower, traditionally the place of Henry VI's murder.

vigil through the night at its altar, and on the following morning received the accolade of Knighthood from the Monarch. This ceremony dates from 1399 and continued until the coronation of King Charles II.

Successive sovereigns were responsible for the many additional buildings that comprise the complex we see today. The inner defensive wall and its thirteen towers were added in the reign of King Henry III (1216-1272) whilst King Edward I (1272-1307) was responsible for the construction of the outer defences, Traitors' Gate, the completion of the Moat (drained in 1843) and the Middle Tower. Legge's Mount and Brass Mount, two bastions on the outer wall, were built in the reign of King Henry VIII.

Traitors' Gate is now seen as an enormous arch below the outer walls, with its portcullis, through which, when this was the main approach from the river, shackled prisoners passed on their final journey.

The delightful Tower Green, where so many visitors today pose for photographs, was not always so pleasant. Described by Macaulay (1800-1859) as "no sadder spot on earth", this was the site of the scaffold where the less common prisoners met their end. Here perished two of King Henry VIII's wives, Anne Boleyn and Catherine Howard. Lady Jane Grey and the Earl of Essex were also executed here.

It was in the Bloody Tower that King Richard III is alleged to have murdered his two young nephews, "the little Princes", in 1483. Sir Walter Raleigh, after being imprisoned here for thirteen years, was beheaded at Westminster in 1618.

The present Chapel Royal of St. Peter ad Vincula was built by King Henry VIII (1509-1547) but its origins date back to the beginning of the twelfth century. Here are buried the remains of Queen Anne Boleyn (1536), Queen Catherine Howard (1542), the Dukes of Northumberland (1553), Somerset (1551) and Monmouth (1685), Lady Jane Grey and her husband, Lord Guildford Dudley (1554), Robert Devereux, Earl of Essex (1601) as well as many others of rank and fame. The organ, originally in the Palace of Westminster, is the oldest remaining in the City of London, dating from 1676. The Chapel is hung with regimental colours and contains many monuments and tombs of historical interest.

For several centuries the Tower of London was the chief arsenal in the kingdom, from which the royal armies and fleets were equipped. At the same time, like other royal palaces, it housed the king's personal armours and weapons. Out of these elements has grown the great historical collection of the Tower Armouries, Britain's national museum of arms and armour. In this development, as in so much of Tower history, Henry VIII was a central figure. Seeking to make England a great military power, he restocked and expanded the arsenal at the Tower. As a connoisseur of fine armour he set up the royal armour workshops at Greenwich which continued to produce armours of the highest quality until the eve of the English Civil War. As

More's cell in the Bell Tower.

Armour made for King Henry VIII, circa 1540 (top) and (bottom) the block and axe.

early as the reign of Elizabeth I the arms and armour of Henry's soldiers and of the king himself were fascinating the select few privileged to visit the Tower.

Most of the public displays are in the White Tower, beginning on the entrance floor with the Hunting and Sporting Gallery. Here may be seen a great variety of specialised weapons developed for use in the hunt, ranging from the small crossbows that shot pellets or stones to bring down birds or rabbits, to the punt gun that could kill a hundred waterfowl at one discharge, and the elephant guns and whaling harpoon-guns. Some of the firearms in the gallery display remarkable technical ingenuity, such as the repeating guns, while others are splendid examples of artistic craftsmanship — guns as works of art. Here special mention should be made of the Monlong pistols, a prized recent acquisition. These flintlock holster pistols with chiselled steel barrels and inlaid silver decoration, were made by Peter Monlong, a Hugenot gunmaker, probably for William III. Visitors interested in firearms will find especially helpful the extended display that illustrates and explains their development from the clumsy matchlock to the self-igniting cartridge rifle.

The Tudor Gallery, on the top floor, is the centrepiece of the entire Armouries, for here are displayed the personal armours of Henry VIII and the armours made in the workshops at Greenwich which he established. As the visitor enters the Gallery he is confronted by the great Greenwich armour made for Henry in his last years. No portrait conveys more powerfully his massive presence. On either side are armours for the foot combat, made in Henry's earlier sunnier years when he was a slim young man of outstanding energy and charm. Further into the gallery are two fine horse armours commissioned by Henry and another said to have been presented to him by the Emperor Maximilian I. Another of the Emperor's presents is the famous ram's horn helmet.

The adjoining Seventeenth-Century Gallery shows how armour gradually disappeared from the battlefield. But beside the equipment of the lancer, light cavalry-man, musketeer and pikeman of the Civil War, are the elegant and ornate personal armours of the Stuarts, with Charles I's engraved and gilt armour outstanding.

The Oriental Gallery, in the Waterloo Building, contains arms and armour from Asia and Africa. The most spectacular exhibits are undoubtedly the elephant armour, captured by Robert Clive at the Battle of Plassey in 1757, which is displayed on a full-size model elephant, and the Japanese Samurai armours, but there are many other pieces worth looking for such as the Indian mortar made in the shape of a sitting tiger, the Burmese dragon gun and the Chinese repeating crossbow.

Bascinet, north Italian, about 1380-1400 (bottom left).

Close helmet from the armour of William Somerset, third Earl of Worcester, made at Greenwich about 1570 (bottom right).

Gilt armour of Charles I (top left).

Henry VIII's tonlet armour (top centre).

Foot combat armour made for Henry VIII at Greenwich, about 1520 (top right).

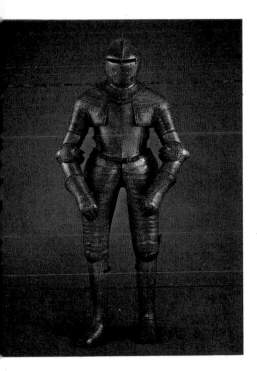

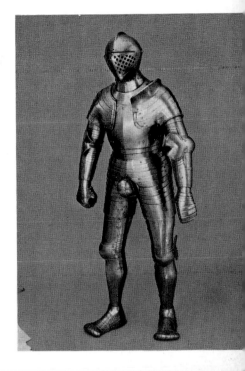

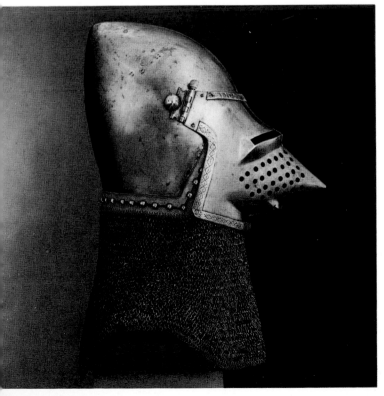

The Crown Jewels.

The Crown Jewels had for many years been kept in the Wakefield Tower but since 1967 have been housed in a specially constructed strongroom below the Waterloo Barracks. Here is probably the world's largest and most valuable collection of jewels and gold plate, comprising the Coronation Regalia, most of which, due to the hatred of everything royal by Oliver Cromwell, dates from 1660. Three notable exceptions are Queen Elizabeth I's salt cellar, which is the oldest of the gold plate, the twelfth-century anointing spoon, and the Ampulla, the age of which cannot be determined for certain, although it is believed to have been used at the Coronation of Henry IV in 1399.

The original Crown of England (St. Edward's Crown) was one of the many treasures destroyed by Cromwell, and the Crown on display today is a copy made for the coronation of King Charles II. The Imperial State Crown, worn by the Monarch at the opening of Parliament and other state occasions, was made by command of Queen Victoria and first used at her coronation in 1838. This is possibly the most valuable crown in the world, containing many precious diamonds, rubies, sapphires and emeralds. Among the many famous and historic stones in this crown are the Stuart Sapphire, the Black Prince's Ruby and the second Star of Africa. The Queen Mother's Crown, made for the coronation of Her Majesty Queen Elizabeth in 1937, contains the famous and beautiful Koh-i-noor diamond, which according to legend, brings misfortune to male owners. This magnificent diamond is the large stone at the centre point of the cross.

Among the splendid objects of royal regalia, the Sovereign's Orb and Sceptre are the most striking and valuable, containing the Great Star of Africa which weighs 530 carats and is the largest cut diamond in the world. Of the many swords displayed, the jewelled Great Sword of State, dating from the late seventeenth century, is undoubtedly the most spectacular. Its scabbard is decorated with diamonds, emeralds, and rubies, in designs forming the Rose of England, the Thistle of Scotland and the Shamrock of Ireland.

On the ground floor are displayed the insignia and robes of the Orders of Knighthood: the Garter, the Bath, St. Michael & St. George, the Victorian Order, the Thistle, St. Patrick, the Star of India, the Indian Empire, and the British Empire. The oldest of these is the Garter founded by Edward III in 1348. According to tradition the King was dancing with Joan of Kent, later the Countess of Salisbury, at a royal ball when to the intense embarrassment of the lady concerned she droppped her garter. With great aplomb the King retrieved it and placed ito on his own leg, stating as he did so, *Honi soit qui mal y pense* ("Shame to him who thinks ill of it") — which was to become the motto of this most noble Order.

The Tower has always been a royal palace and under the direct control of the Sovereign who appoints the Constable

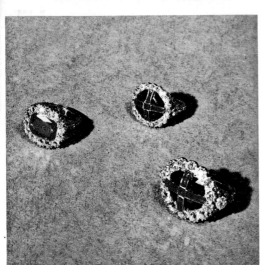

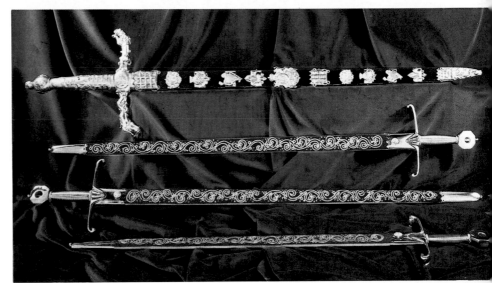

The Anointing Spoon and Ampulla (top left). The Coronation Rings (centre left). The Sovereign's Orb and Sceptre (top right). Queen Elizabeth, the Queen Mother's Crown (bottom left). Swords of State (centre right). The Imperial State Crown (bottom right).

The Imperial Crown of India (top left).

Queen Elizabeth's Salt (top centre).

Ceremonial State Maces (top right).

Golden Spurs and Bracelets made for Charles II (below).

St. Edward's Crown (facing page).

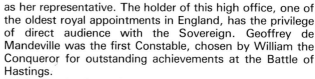

Resident Governor inspecting Yeomen Warders on parade.

The Yeoman Gaoler.

as her representative. The holder of this high office, one of the oldest royal appointments in England, has the privilege of direct audience with the Sovereign. Geoffrey de Mandeville was the first Constable, chosen by William the Conqueror for outstanding achievements at the Battle of Hastings.

Originally, the Constable was appointed for life, but since 1933 the term of office has been five years. From the reign of Elizabeth I the Lieutenant assumed command of the Tower on the Constable's behalf but in time the Lieutenant too no longer resided in the Tower. Nowadays routine administration is in the hands of the Resident Governor and Major, who is also the Keeper of the Jewel House (a Royal appointment), assisted by two Deputy Governors. The Governor, or one of his deputies, is obliged to be present in the Tower at all times. The Governor also has under his command the military guard and those much loved Yeomen Warders, who should not be confused with the Yeomen of the Guard despite the general similarity of uniform. The splendid Tudor style State Dress of the Yeomen Warders was approved in its present form in Queen Victoria's reign. It is reserved for ceremonial duty and the guarding of royalty during visits to the City of London. The State Dress consists of a Tudor bonnet with a red, white and blue ribbon around the base of the crown, white neck ruff, scarlet uniform with gold embroidered Royal Crown, Tudor rose, thistle, shamrock and leek on front and back, with the royal cypher. The skirt, which finishes just below the knee, has double lines of gold braid on either side of a black velvet strip, as do the belt and sleeves. Scarlet breeches and stockings with black shoes are worn with tri-colour rosettes at the knee and on the shoes. The Warders, when in state dress, are armed with eight-foot-long partizans bearing the royal arms and cypher. They are more usually seen in their dark blue undress uniforms which were approved by Queen Victoria in 1858. The Yeomen Warders are a unique body by tradition originating from the reign of Henry VII. They now number some forty men, carefully selected ex-warrant officers, who, in the words of a former Constable, the Duke of Wellington, must be "deserving, gallant, and meritorious discharged sergeants of the Army", though in the course of time selection has been enlarged to include the Royal Air Force and Royal Marines. Most of the Warders are married and live with their wives and children in various quarters situated throughout the Tower. The principal responsibility of the Warders has always been for the security of the Tower. Once they looked after is prisoners; now they attend to the three million visitors who come to the Tower every year to whom they are affectionately known as the "Beefeaters" (although it should be noted that this is not a complimentary form of address), the smartly uniformed guides and courteous "nursemaids" who never lose their patience and rarely complain at being asked to pose for the never-ending photographs!

The Chief Yeoman Warder, who on ceremonial occasion carries a silver mace topped by a replica of the White Tower, is responsible for securing the gates of the Tower which begins the nightly ritual of the Ceremony of the Keys. The Chief Warder's second-in-command is the Yeoman Gaoler who bears the ceremonial axe. Other titled Warders are the Yeoman Clerk, Sexton to the Chapels Royal, and the Yeoman Raven Master, who is in charge of those unofficial custodians of the Tower, the half-a-dozen or so ravens. The Governor, as Keeper of the Jewel House, is aided by a Curator with a separate staff of Assistant Curators and Wardens. The Wardens wear a distinctive Royal Household uniform of dark blue frock coat with gold epaulettes and a black top hat with a gold band. The Tower's administrative team includes the Master of the Armouries, assisted by the Keeper of Armour, the Keeper of Firearms and the Keeper of Edged Weapons, all very specialist posts held by internationally recognised experts in their particular fields. To cater for the needs of an ever increasing number of schoolchildren (well over 100,000 come every year on organised

Plaque marking the site of the public scaffold in Trinity Gardens, Tower Hill.

The Yeoman Raven Master.

Yeomen Warders in ceremonial procession.

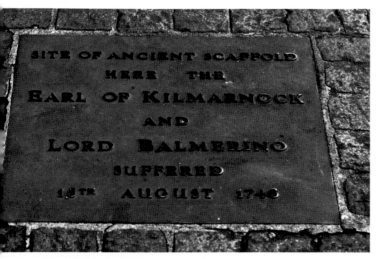

The Chief Yeoman Warder with his mace of office.

The Golden Keys of the Tower.

The Ceremony of the Keys — "The Challenge" (above) — and (below) the conclusion of the ceremony.

visits) and adult students, an Education Officer was appointed in 1974.

Since the regular army was formed after the restoration of Charles II there has always been a military guard at the Tower. Nowadays the guard is usually provided by one of the Foot Guards regiments, whose men are instantly recognizable by their bearskins. The changing of the Guard, at Queen's House, usually takes place each day at about 11.30 a.m. But another regiment, the Royal Fusiliers, have an even closer link with the Tower, for the regiment was raised here in the reign of James II, by the Constable of the Tower, Lord Dartmouth. Recently, the Fusiliers' headquarters and officers' mess have been re-established in the Tower, along with the regimental museum which tells the Fusilier's proud story through portraits, documents, medals and uniforms and battle dioramas.

No other historic monument in England can boast such an unbroken continuity with the past or have played such a major role in the nation's heritage. The Tower's great sense of history lives on in its traditions and particularly in the ceremonies which are still performed here virtually unchanged after several centuries.

The Tower is justly well-known for its unique Ceremony of the Keys which in some form may well have been enacted nightly for over seven hundred years, since the defences of the Tower were completed. This is probably the oldest military ceremony in the world and no-one can witness it without admiring the absolute precision of the participants or fail to be stirred by tremendous feelings of history. The ceremony begins at eight minutes to ten o'clock each evening when the Chief Yeoman Warder, in a long scarlet coat, leaves the Byward tower accompanied by an escort of four soldiers and secures the main gates of the Tower. Then, as he and the escort return, the sentry at the Bloody Tower gives the challenge, "Halt, who goes there?" The Chief Warder replies, "The Keys". Sentry, "Whose keys?" Chief Warder, "Queen Elizabeth's Keys". The party then proceeds to the foot of the steps leading to Broad Walk where they are met by the main guard who present arms. The Chief Warder, raising his Tudor bonnet, cries out, "God preserve Queen Elizabeth". The guard respond with "Amen" as the clock strikes ten, and the bugler then sounds the Last Post. The Chief Warder finally bears the keys to the Queen's House where are kept securely overnight.

Canary Wharf.

View over Millwall Dock towards Glengall Bridge. ▷

St. Catherine's Dock. Built by Thomas Telford in 1826.

ST PAUL'S CATHEDRAL

Sir Christopher Wren's materpiece stands on a site occupied by several predecessors, the last of which perished in the Great Fire of London in 1666. The building of the present Cathedral commenced in 1675 and the last stone was laid in 1710. Acclaimed by many authorities as one of the most beautiful Renaissance buildings in the world, its dome is only surpassed in size by St Peter's in Rome.

The inner dome is decorated by paintings by Sir James Thornhill depicting the life of St Paul, and above it there is the larger outer dome constructed of wood covered with lead. Visitors are strongly recommended to make the ascent to the Whispering Gallery in order to experience the acoustic phenomenon from which it gets its name, and thence on to the exterior Stone Gallery from where the whole of London is visible. Those with sufficient stamina may continue higher yet, up to the Golden Gallery and then finally into the Golden Ball itself on which the Golden Cross dominates the City of London.

The magnificent interior of the Cathedral contains many fine paintings, sculptures, monuments and works of art, foremost of which are the original choir stalls carved by Wren's contemporary, Grinling Gibbons, the fine wrought iron work by Tijou, another contemporary, the new High Altar based on Wren's own design and dedicated to Commonwealth troops who died in the Second World War, and the American Memorial Chapel in the apse behind the Altar. One object which miraculously survived the Great Fire is the macabre statue of John Donne the poet. Also here are Holman Hunt's copy of his famous painting *The Light of the World,* memorials to artists Turner, Reynolds, Van Dyck, Millais, Constable, and Blake; soldiers Sir John Moore, General Gordon, Lord Kitchener and the mighty sarcophagus of the Duke of Wellington. Lord Nelson's remains are interred in a black marble sarcophagus made originally for Henry VIII, whilst those of the master architect lie in the crypt with the simple inscription *Si Monumentum requiris circumspice* (If you seek a memorial, look around you).

The nave, looking east. ▷

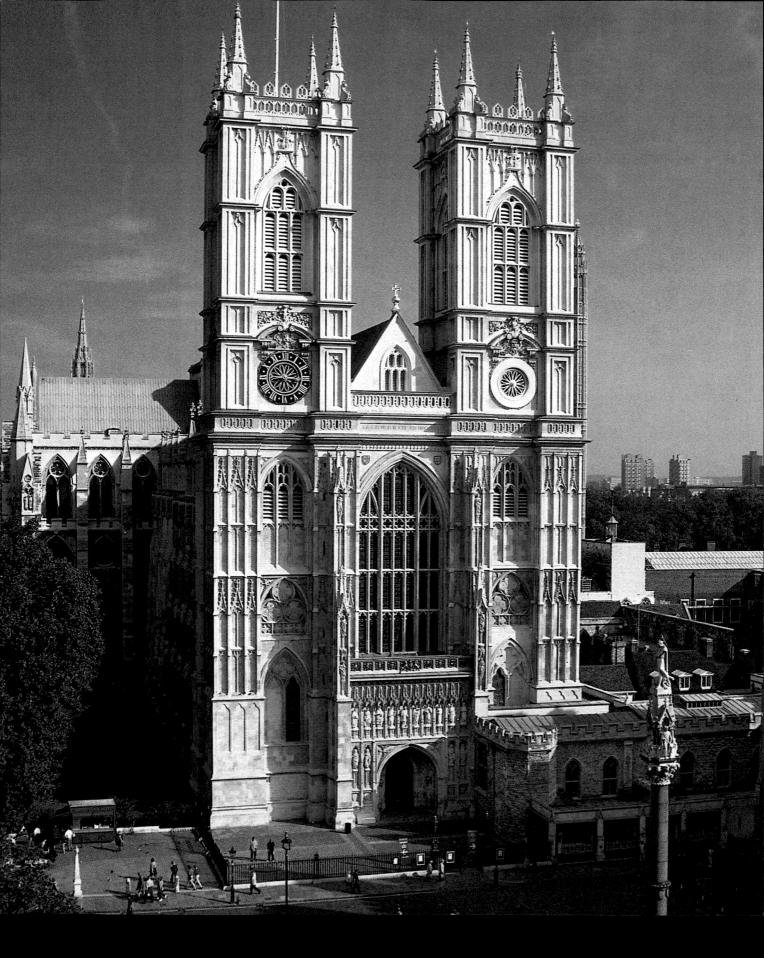

The best known view of the Abbey: the West Door.

The tomb of the Unknown Warrior.

WESTMINSTER ABBEY

One of the finest examples of Early English Gothic architecture, founded by Edward the Confessor in 1065 on the site of a church which had been built 500 years earlier. "The Abbey", as it is affectionately known to the English, but more properly the Collegiate Church of St. Peter in Westminster, was mostly built in the thirteenth century during the reign of Henry III.

Entering by the west door the gaze is directed upwards to the vaulted ceiling, then along the great nave lit by the aisle and clerestory windows above. Despite the advice often given to ignore the clutter of memorials, these testimonials to the great dead are the very stuff of which history is made. This is where all the English monarchs have been crowned for over 600 years and many of them subsequently buried, their magnificent tombs surrounded by a proliferation of commoners — prime ministers, artists, physicians, poets, actors, authors, soldiers and sailors, politicians. Holding pride of place is the tomb of the Unknown Warrior, just inside the west door, commemorating the nation's dead of all ranks and Services, nearly a million who perished in the First World War.

Among the famous persons buried or commemorated here are Queen Elizabeth I; the tragic Mary, Queen of Scots, beheaded in 1587 by order of her cousin and reburied in the Abbey 25 years later by command of her son, King James I; King George II (the last sovereign to be buried in the Abbey); *Soldiers:* Field Marshal Allenby, General Gordon, Lord Baden-Powell; *Scientists:* Sir Isaac Newton, Darwin; *Writers:* Thackeray, Ruskin, Goldsmith, Burns, Wordsworth, Browning, Milton, Chaucer, Ben Jonson (incorrectly spelt Johnson), Samuel Johnson, Dickens, Shakespeare; *Musicians:* Handel, Purcell; *Statesmen:* Disraeli, Chamberlain, Gladstone, Palmerston, Fox, Pitt; *Actors:* Irving, Garrick; and *Painter:* Kneller (the only painter so honoured), and many, many others.

The Abbey's founder is buried in the Chapel of Edward the Confessor where his time-worn tomb was for hundreds of years a place of pilgrimage. The tomb's outer covering of gold and precious stones was stripped during the Reformation as was the original silver head from the nearby effigy of Herny V.

The Chapel also contains the tombs of Henry VIII, Edward I and his wife Eleanor of Castile, Edward III, Richard II (his portrait, the earliest contemporary painting of an English King, hangs in the nave by the west door), Philippa of Hainault and Anne of Bohemia.

The nave, looking west.

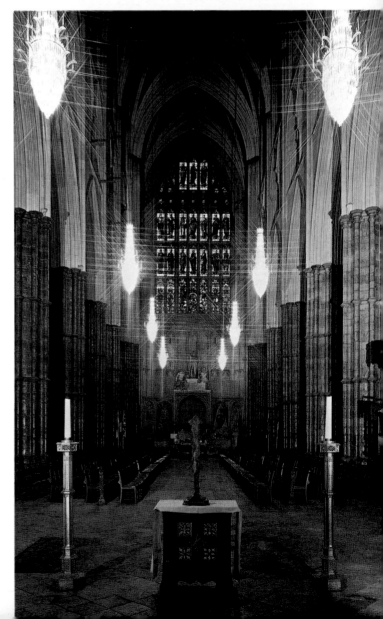

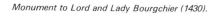

The most sumptuous single addition to the Abbey is unquestionably Henry VII's Chapel at the eastern end, described by a contemporary antiquary, John Leland, as one of the wonders of the world. Henry was buried here in 1509 alongside his Queen, Elizabeth of York, who six years before had died in childbirth. The delicate lacework tracery of the fan-vaulted ceiling is unparalleled in the whole of England.

The octagonal Chapter House, dating from the midthirteenth century, has seen endless restorations, though much of the original fabric remains along with the floor tiles which surprisingly have survived to this day. On the plain stone benches around the walls sat the medieval monks at their business. For over one hundred and fifty years the Chapter House was used as Parliament House, until 1547 when King Edward VI allowed the House of Commons to meet in St. Stephens Chapel in the old Palace of Westminster. Thereafter the Chapter House fell into disuse until 1860 when major restorations were carried out by Sir George Gilbert Scott. The Coronation Chair is situated between the High Altar and the Chapel of Edward the Confessor. The oak chair which was built by order of Edward I in 1300 to contain the legendary Stone of Scone, captured four years earlier in Scotland, has been used for every Coronation since 1308.

Visitors would also be well advised to see the Museum and the adjacent Chapel of the Pyx which in ancient times was used as the Royal Treasury. Here was kept the Pyx, a box containing standard coins of the realm against which current gold and silver coins were tested each year for weight and purity of metal.

St. Margaret's, nearby Westminster Abbey. St Margaret's has been the parish church of the House of Commons since 1614. According to tradition the original church was founded by Edward the Confessor in the twelfth century but the present building dates from 1523. The fine Flemish glass of the east window was a betrothal present from Ferdinand and Isabella of Spain to Prince Arthur, son of Henry VII, and their daughter, Catharine of Aragon. Unfortunately poor Arthur died and his brother, later to become Henry VIII, had married his widowed sister-in-law before the gift arrived. It was not until 1758 that the glass was installed in St. Margaret's. Among the famous persons buried here are Sir Walter Raleigh, William Caxton, and Admiral Hollar Blake. Those married here include Samuel Pepys (1655), John Milton (1656) and Winston Churchill (1908).

Queen Anne's Gate, Westminster. A street of early eighteenth-century houses of brown brickwork and bright clean paintwork. Now mainly used for commercial purposes the houses are remarkably well preserved. Elaborate doors, wooden porches, elegant canopies, black iron railings, torch extinguishers (No. 26) and the statue of Queen Anne outside No. 13 make this one of the prettiest streets in London.

The Coronation Chair and the Stone of Scone.

King Henry VIII's Chapel.

THE HOUSES OF PARLIAMENT

Dominating the eastern extremity of the complex of buildings known as the Houses of Parliament, but more correctly the Palace of Westminster, is the 320 foot high tower housing the Palace clock. Famed throughout the world as Big Ben (actually the name of the bell), it was reputedly so called after Sir Benjamin Hall, the burly Commissioner of Works when it was installed in 1858. A light above the clock signifies that the House of Commons is sitting during the night, whilst during the day the Union Jack is flown from the Victoria Tower.

This has been the seat of government since the early part of the eleventh century but not until 1547 did it become the permanent home of Parliament. The present neo-Gothic buildings, dating from about 1850, are the work of Sir Charles Barry and Augustus Pugin replacing the earlier structure which was almost totally destroyed by fire in a single night on 16 October 1834. The medieval crypt and cloisters of St. Stephen's Chapel escaped the fire and were skifully incorporated into the new building along with Westminster Hall which for six hundred years was the chief court of English Law. This great hall, with its fine timber roof spanning some 70 feet, was originally built by William Rufus in 1097 and restored by King Richard II in 1398. It has been the scene of much stirring history — from Coronation banquets to trials for high treason. It was here that Sir Thomas More, King Charles I, William Wallace, Guy Fawkes, the Earl of Essex and many others of high rank were sentenced to death.

The never-to-be-forgotten Gunpowder Plot of 1605 failed to blow up the Houses of Parliament but enemy bombing in 1941 inflicted serious damage to the Commons. Much of the timber used in the reconstruction of the new chamber, opened in 1950, was given by Commonwealth countries.

The House of Lords, which providentially escaped the 1941 bombing is a sumptuous chamber in rich tones of red and gold and is the meeting place of the Lords Spiritual and the Lords Temporal. The walls are lined with paintings and with statues of the eighteen barons who secured the Magna Car-

*Westminster
Bridge.*

ta from King John in 1215. At the south end of the chamber is the magnificent Queen's Throne with its beautiful carved and gilt canopy — the smaller throne on the right is for the Consort. The Lord Chancellor, who presides over the assembly, sits on the Woolsack which signifies the former importance of wool to the economy of England.

The genius of Pugin's ornamentation in the grand Gothic style is richly portrayed in the Queen's Robing Room, a sumptuous state apartment replete with elaborate woodcarving and containing a series of paintings by William Dyce depicting the legend of King Arthur. The adjacent Royal Gallery, a long room with a fine coloured Minton tiled floor,

is dominated by two huge paintings, *The Death of Nelson* and *The Meeting of Wellington and Blucher after Waterloo*, by Daniel Maclise, and contains gilt statues of every monarch from King Alfred to Queen Anne.

The State Opening of Parliament is an annual event, usually towards the end of October or early November or following a general election. The Queen drives from Buckingham Palace in the Irish State Coach, accompanied by a sovereign's mounted escort, by way of The Mall to the House of Lords. The Queen's Speech from the throne in the House of Lords (the sovereign has not been admitted to the Commons for over three hundred years since King Charles I

Big Ben and Queen Boadicea.

Lambeth Bridge.

was refused entry), traditionally sets the theme of the Governments's business for the ensuing session.

The graceful cast-iron *Westminster Bridge* was constructed between 1854-62 to replace the earlier one of stone.

The design blends well with the neo-Gothic of the Houses of Parliament. At the south end of the bridge is the bronze statue of Queen Boadicea by Thomas Thornycroft, unveiled in 1902. Boadicea, widow of the King of Iceni, rebelled against the Roman occupation and in A.D. 61 attacked the City which was razed to the ground and most of its inhabitants were slain. The professionally traImed and better armed Roman army subsequently proved superior to the Britons who were slaughtered without mercy. Boadicea and her daughters took poison to avoid a more terrible death.

Statue of Sir Winston Churchill in Parliament Square.

The Royal Gallery.

The House of Commons
(bottom).

N.º 10 Downing Street.

Cabinet Room.

Whitehall is the street linking Trafalgar Square to Parliament Square and is known for its concentration of Government offices and historic buildings: Ministry of Defence, Ministry of Agriculture, the Home Office, the Treasury, the old Admiralty Building, the Lord Privy Seal's office, Horse Guards, the Banqueting Hall, and at the far end the Cenotaph.

The Banqueting Hall, designed by Inigo Jones in 1619 for King James I, is all that remains of Whitehall Palace. One of the first of London's buildings in the classical Italian tradition it was possibly also the first to be built of Portland stone. Rubens received 3,000 pounds and a knighthood from King Charles I for the nine allegorical paintings which adorn the ceiling. Possibly the King saw the paintings on that icy cold January morning when he left the House by way of a first floor window on the way to the scaffold. Oliver Cromwell made much use of the Hall for the reception of visiting ambassadors and King Charles II was officially welcomed here by the House of Commons on his Restoration. Opposite is the more colourful *Horse Guards,* built between 1750 and 1760 to the design of William Kent on the site of the guardhouse to the Whitehall Palace. Here are to be found those very popular subjects for the tourists' photographs: the imperturbable mounted guard of the Household Cavalry.

Horse Guards Parade, the former tilt-yard of the old Palace, is on the other side of the central archway and there the annual ceremony of Trooping the Colour takes place on the soverign's official birthday.

Changing the Guard is another colourful ceremony which takes place most mornings in the courtyard of the Horse Guards, Whitehall, by the Queen's Life Guard from the Household Cavalry. At Buckingham Palace the guard is changed by the Queen's Guard, provided by the Guards division.

Downing Street, off Whitehall is undoubtedly the most famous street in London, for No. 10 is the official home of the Prime Minister and has been since Sir Robert Walpole took up residence in 1735 at the suggestion of King George II. No. 11 is occupied by the Chancellor of the Exchequer whilst No. 12 is the office of the government Chief Whip.

Trooping the Colour.

POMP, PAGEANTRY AND CEREMONIES

No ceremony is more popular than the ancient and mysterious ceremony of *Trooping the Colour.* This splendid and colourful event in honour of the Soverign's official birthday is held annually on the first or second Saturday in June.

The route from Buckingham Palace to Horse Guards Parade, behind Whitehall, is decorated with banners and flags and lined with thousands of spectators, eagerly waiting to see the Queen heading the procession, dressed in uniform and riding side-saddle on one of her favourite horses.

The troops, in full dress uniforms, are from the Household Cavalry and the Guards Division. Two separate mounted regiments make up the Corps of Household Cavalry; the Life Guards originating from the time of King Charles I, who wear scarlet tunics with white plumed helmets, and the Blues and Royals (formerly the Royal Horse Guards) with blue tunics and red plumed helmets, who were a regiment during the Cromwellian period. These regiments share the honour of providing a personal bodyguard for the Sovereign on all state occasions.

Five separate regiments comprise the Guards Division, all of whom wear scarlet tunics and bearskins: the Grenadiers (1656); the Coldstream (1650); the Scots Guards (1642); the Irish Guards (1900) and youngest regiment, the Welsh Guards (1915). The Guards also perform guard duties at Buckingham Palace, St. James's Palace and Clarence House.

The sheer mass of dazzling colour the music of the mounted bands, the precision marching and counter-marching, are truly an experience never to be forgotten.

The Life Guards with scarlet tunics and white plumed helmets.

Sentry on duty, member of the Scots Guards.

Horse Guards Building, Whitehall.

Horse Guards.

Changing of the Guard, Horse Guards Building.

Mounted sentries at Horse Guards are provided by troopers of the Life Guard (left) and (right) the Blues and Royals.

St. James's Palace: the Tudor Gatehouse.

St. James's Palace: the Chapel Royal.

BUILDINGS: HISTORICAL AND CONTEMPORARY

Despite the extensive development that has changed London's pre-war skyline almost beyond recognition, the best of its administrative, commercial, and domestic building is more historical than modern.

St. James's Palace was the sovereign's London residence until supplanted by Buckingham Palace, and its former importance is still acknowledged by the fact that foreign ambassadors are accredited to the "Court of St. James's". King Henry VIII demolished the Norman leper hospital originally occupying the site and built himself a royal palace, of which there remains today only the fine brick gatetower, Guard Room, the Presence Chamber and the Chapel Royal, which has a magnificent painted ceiling attributed to Holbein. There are two Chapels Royal attached to the Palace, the second is in nearby Marlborough Gate, known as the Queen's Chapel after Henrietta Maria, wife of King Charles I. Designed by Inigo Jones (*circa* 1627), this little-known architectural treasure is of classical proportions with an ornate roof, Carolean panelling and royal pews.

Across the river from the Houses of Parliament are the new buildings of St. Thomas's Hospital, founded in 1213 and moved to this site in 1868. Beyond the hospital, by Lambeth Bridge, is the irregular shape of Lambeth Palace, the official London residence of the Archbishops of Canterbury for over 750 years. The red brick gatehouse was built by Bishop Morton in about 1495 and is a superb example of early Tudor brickwork. The Great Hall, largely destroyed during the time of Cromwell, was rebuilt by Archbischop Juxon in 1663. The hall has a magnificent hammer-beam roof and contains an important library with some finely illuminated manuscripts. The Lollards' Tower, *circa* 1450, supposedly commemorates the followers of John Wycliffe (1320-1384). The undercroft, or vaulted crypt, below the Chapel is the oldest part of the Palace dating from the early thirteenth century, whilst the Chapel itself has been extensively restored as the result of severe damage during the last war. The Guard Room has a fourteenth-century timber roof and contains a rich collection of paintings, including portraits by Holbein and Van Dyck. Nearby the south gateway is the parish church of St. Mary, which was rebuilt in 1851. Only the Kentish ragstone west tower remains from the earlier fourteenth-century building.

Beyond the elegant bridge at Richmond is Hampton Court, which Cardinal Wolsey, no doubt in an effort to halt his fall from favour, presented to King Henry VIII but, as history re-cords, to no avail. Built between 1515 and 1520 as Wolsey's private residence, this was to become the most beautiful royal palace in the land. Sucessive royal occupants enlarged it; first Henry VIII who added the Great Hall, Chapel and laid the first tennis court in England. Henry VIII broght five of his wives in turn to live here as Queen and according to legend the ghosts of two of them, Jane Seymour and Catherine Howard, still haunt the Palace. King Edward VI, Mary Tudor, Queen Elizabeth I, King James I, King Charles I (it was both his home and his prison) and King Charles II held court here. The next major reconstruction was carried out by Sir Christopher Wren during the reign of King William and Queen Mary. The Wren additions include the Fountain Court and garden front. Through the second courtyard and over the Anne Boleyn Gateway is the curious astronomical clock erected in 1540 and still in working order. The Great Vine is

Lambeth Palace and the parish church of St. Mary.

St. Bride's.

St. Dunstan-in-the-West.

Queen Elizabeth I.

Brompton Oratory.

St. Clement Danes.

Doctor Johnson.

Westminster Cathedral. ▷

Madame Tussaud's and the
Planetarium.

Queen Elizabeth I.

King Henry VIII and his six
wives.

Buckingham Palace.

The Queen's Guards Parade.

Buckingham Palace: the Throne Room.

reputed to have been planted in 1769 and the famous Maze, 6 feet high and 2 feet thick, probably dates from the reign of King William and Queen Mary.

The Palace's art collection includes such masterpieces as Titian's *Jacopo Sannazaro* (Portrait of a Man), *Apollo and the Nine Muses* by Tintoretto, Correggio's *Virgin and Child,* a rare religious painting by Holbein, *Noli me Tangere* and Bellini's *Portrait of a Man* as well as major works by Van Dyck, Lely and Kneller.

Madame Tussaud's, Marylebone, NW1, is the world famous waxworks established here about 1833 when some of its first exhibits included deathmasks of guillotine victims from the French Revolution. Here the visitor may wander through the pages of history and mingle with the famous and infamous. An international display of Kings, Queens, politicians, stars of films, television and pop, sportsmen and women, all portrayed with an uncanny realism.

Next door, under a green copper dome, is *The Planetarium,* where the wonders of the heavens are displayed by means of an ingenious projector, accompanied by an interesting commentary.

Buckingham Palace, the building known to all as the Queen's official London home, is a mixture of old and new. The original house built for the Duke of Buckingham in 1703 was substantially remodelled by John Nash in Palladian style 125 years later. The façade facing the Mall was added by Sir Aston Webb as recently as 1913. On her succession to the throne in 1837, Queen Victoria made Buckingham Palace her permanent home — the first monarch to do so — and instituted the custom by which the Royal Standard is flown from the flagstaff to show that the sovereign is in residence.

The Queen's Gallery (entrance in Buckingham Palace Road) is open to the public and presents an ever-changing display of art treasures from the royal collection. Behind the Palace

Buckingham
Palace: the
Entrée Stairs.

The Wellington Arch.

is the Royal Mews where the horses and coaches used on state occasions are stabled. Here kept the Irish State Coach, used for state openings of Parliament, which was bought by Queen Victoria in 1852; the Golden State coach designed for King George III and used for coronations; the Glass State coach of King George V used for royal weddings; along with a fascinating collection of barouches, landaus, carriages and a unique display of harnesses and trappings.

The elaborate Victoria Memorial in front of Buckingham Palace, the Mall and Admiralty Arch were all part of the nation's tribute to Queen Victoria, constructed between 1910-12. The Memorial comprises a seated figure of the Queen looking towards the Mall surrounded by several symbolic groups surmounted by the gilt winged figure of Victory supported by Courage and Constancy. The Mall is the wide tree-lined driveway linking Buckingham Palace with Trafalgar Square and is the best vantage point for viewing royal processions. Spanning the entrance to the Mall from Trafalgar Square is Admiralty Arch through the centre of which only the sovereign may pass.

Albert Memorial.

Royal Albert Hall.

Telecom Tower.

Albert Hall, Kensington Gore, was the pride of Victorian London ·and named after Queen Victoria's consort, the Royal Albert Hall of Arts and Sciences. The elliptical domed building, completed in 1871, has a capacity of approximately 8,000 and now serves a variety of purposes, the most popular-despite its somewhat imperfect acoustics-being the annual Promenade Concerts founded by Sir Henry Wood. *Telecom Tower,* Howland Street, W1 formerly was London's highest building, nearly 600 feet above ground level. Its purpose is to allow telecommunications uninterrupted by other modern tall buildings.

THE PARKS AND SQUARES

Looking at a map the emerald pathes of London's parks stand out like islands in the very centre of its vast sea of streets and buildings. Islands where the visitor may stroll at leisure oblivious of the frantic activity beyond. Nowhere better for this than *Hyde Park,* a delightful expanse of grass and woodland covering some 360 acres.

Rennies bridge across the Serpentine informally divides Hyde Park from *Kensington Gardens,* once the grounds of Kensington Palace.

St. James's Park is by far the prettiest, and the oldest of the royal parks and is a joy to walk in at any season of the year. *Green Park,* added to St. James's Park by King Charles II, is the smallest royal park in central London. Consisting mainly of grassland and trees It is a peaceful haven from Piccadilly's traffic.

If one is looking for all that is to be desired in a park then *Regent's Park* succeeds admirably. John Nash, who also re-modelled St. James's Park, designed Regent's Park and it was named thus in honour of the Prince Regent (later to become King George IV) and first opened to the public in 1838.

The Zoological Gardens at the north end of the park are a great favourite with children, especially Pet's Corner, and one may be forgiven for overlooking that its principal objective is scientific.

Grosvenor Square is named after Sir Richard Grosvenor, a wealthy landowner, who developed the site towards the end of the eighteenth century. One of the oldest of London's squares, it is dominated today by the modern-

Trafalgar Square, the true heart of London.

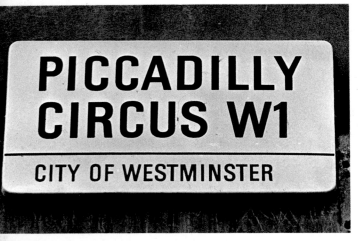

style American Embassy which takes up the whole of the west side.

Leicester Square, surrounded by cinemas and restaurants takes its name from the second Earl of Leicester who had a house on the north side in 1631. The present square dates from 1874 when it was laid out by Albert Grant who also provided the central white marble fountain and statue of Shakespeare.

Trafalgar Square commemorating Nelson's naval victory of 1805, was designed by Sir Charles Barry, and laid out between 1829 and 1841. Commanding the square is Nelson's column, a fluted granite shaft nearly 185 feet high topped by another 17 feet of E.H. Baily's statue of England's greatest

Piccadilly Circus: the once-called "hub of the Empire".

Travel: overground and Underground.

naval hero. The four bronze lions at the column's base are the work of Sir Edwin Landseer and were not placed until 1868, some 26 years after the column was erected.

The fountains and friendly pigeons make Trafalgar Square a popular rendezvous for Londoner and tourist alike, whilst its sheer size and central position provides a focal point for political demonstrations and public meetings.

Piccadilly Circus at night is a blaze of colour from the huge animated neon advertisements. Situated at the centre of London's entertainment world in the West End it is a great attraction to tourists who are drawn to it by some mysterious force — perhaps by the statue of Eros affectionately thought of as the god of love, but in reality an aluminium portrayal of the Angel of Christian Charity, erected in 1893 as a tribute to that great Victorian philanthropist, the Earl of Shaftesbury.

GETTING ABOUT

An increasing number of London's visitors arrive by air at Heathrow, one of the world's busiest international airports, now conveniently connected to the capital by means of the Piccadilly Line.

Also visitor's arrive from mainland Europe on the Eurostar train service from Paris & Brussels into Waterloo.

The best way of exploring London is as a pedestrian roaming from any one of a dozen centres, but for the longer journey a wide choice of London's red buses is available, as well as the equally famous black taxis, both an established part of the London scene. The Underground (much of it *above* ground in fact, though *not* overhead) serves the whole metropolis and has the added atraction of being free from road traffic jams. The Circle line offers a two-way

Fortnum and Mason (top) and Covent Garden (bottom and right).

route conveniently enabling the visitor to reach many places of interest. London Transport runs regular sightseeing bus tours and conducted coach tours to the more popular tourist attractions in and around London and issue excellent descriptive guide books, leaflets, and maps.

Harrods, shopping mecca of the world. ▷

Selfridges, Oxford Street.

Gieves & Hawkes.

SHOPPING, EATING AND ENTERTAINMENT

Serious shopping or just browsing are equally rewarding experiences in London whose range of shops, stores, and stalls cater for all tastes — and purses. Carnaby Street achieved fame overnight in the late 1960's when it became the mecca of ultra-modern fashion and its influence rapidly spread throughout the capital, and indeed the world, as evidenced by the now common-place boutiques specialising in clothes for young people. *Haute couture,* exclusive and expensive, is to be found in and around fashionable Mayfair and Knightsbridge, whilst inbetween tastes are well served by the Marks & Spencer stores, justifiably well-known for their consistently good value in an increasingly wide range of goods. Regent Street, New Bond Street, and Burlington Arcade offer the best in expensive jewellery, as does Jermyn Street in mens' wear.

Shopping in the exclusive Harrods store in Knightsbridge is not necessarily expensive and its ability to supply every possible demand – well almost – has made it legendary. Oxford Street is all shops with a preponderance selling nothing but footwear and is also the home of several departmental stores including Selfridge's, Debenhams, D.H. Evans and John Lewis.

Old and new books are a speciality of Hatchards in Piccadilly and others are in Charing Cross Road led by Foyles ("the biggest bookshop in the world"). Art dealers of all kinds abound in St. James's, Knightsbridge, and Bond Street, and the auction rooms of Sotheby's, Christie's, and others offer excitement and interest.

Not to be missed are the colourful street markets (there are nearly 100 of them in London) where the entertainment is free and bargains abound. A very pleasant Sunday morning can be spent just wandering around Petticoat Lane (Middlesex Street) in London's East End and the neighbouring Club Row (Sclater Street) where children especially will be enthralled by the animals on sale — all kinds, shapes and sizes. Leather Lane (Holborn) is a weekday general market where household goods, fruit and vegetables are sold or if we believe the stallholders, given away! The antique bargain hunter should try his luck in Portobello Road, W10 or Camden Passage, Islington where the speciality is antiques — mostly old and genuine but with the inevitable sprinkling of the reproduction.

In the heart of the City, Leadenhall market originally sold poultry but now also offers a variety of groceries and greengroceries.

You have to be an early riser to see the meat market at Smithfield or Spitalfields meat market in action. Both are essentially wholesale but there is a certain amount of retail business in the surrounding areas. The vegetable, fruit and flower market centred on Convent Garden for hundreds of years now has a new home at Nime Elms on the South Bank.

When it comes to eating the choice is endless. The ubiquitous sandwich is available at numerous coffee-bars or from that great British establishment, the pub, which can take the form of the chromium plated ultra-modern to the red plush and mirrored old tavern, or a peculiar compromise of the two. Light refreshments can be had at most pubs and many have excellent restaurants. Beer, that uniquely English drink, be it the sharp tasting pale golden bitter or the sweeter dark brown ale goes down well with a ploughman's lunch (crusty bread, butter, cheese and pickles).

Specialities of London's East End are the nearly instant and very nutritious fish and chips, and a wide range of sea foods (jellied eels, whelks, cockles, shrimps, crab, lobster and mussels) still sold from roadside stalls. All the large department stores have restaurant facilities and a choice of international cuisine is available from a multitude of hotels and restaurants in the West End.

A tremendous variety of entertainment is available; theatres, cinemas, discotheques, gambling (now legalised), the racy strip-clubs of Soho, music concerts on the South Bank, at the Wigmore Hall, the Royal Albert Hall or in the summer months by the lake in the open air at Kenwood. Ballet and opera at the Coliseum and Covent Garden. For the sporting enthusiast there is a choice of football, tennis, ice-skating, fishing, boating, sailing, swimming, bowling (indoor and outdoor), skiing on artificial slopes, greyhound racing, and riding.

SHERLOCK HOLMES

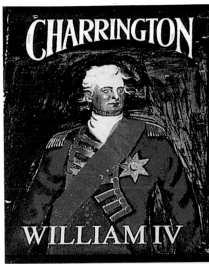

CHARRINGTON

WILLIAM IV

THE TWO BREWERS

KINGS ARMS

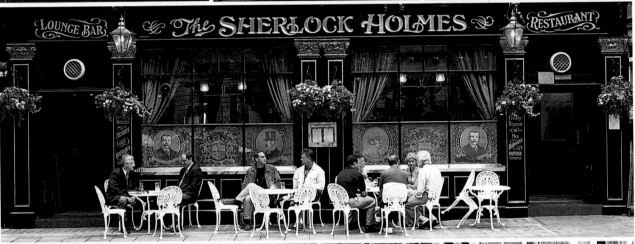

LOUNGE BAR — *The* SHERLOCK HOLMES — RESTAURANT

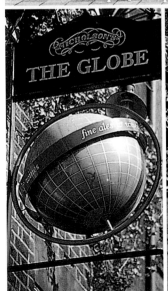

NICHOLSON'S
THE GLOBE

fine ales

The Fitzroy Tavern

TAYLOR WALKER

THE PLOUGH

FULLER'S

ALE & PIE

HOUSE

The JACK HORNER

Aerial view of Windsor Castle.

The Queen's Audience Chamber.

The Wheel.

The London Eye.
The giant observation
wheel stands on the
south bank in Jubilee
Gardens.
It has been operational
since 2000 and provides
breathtaking views across
London up to a distance
of 45 km. It takes 30
minutes to revolve at a
speed of 0.26 mph. It is
now established as one of
London's major
attractions.

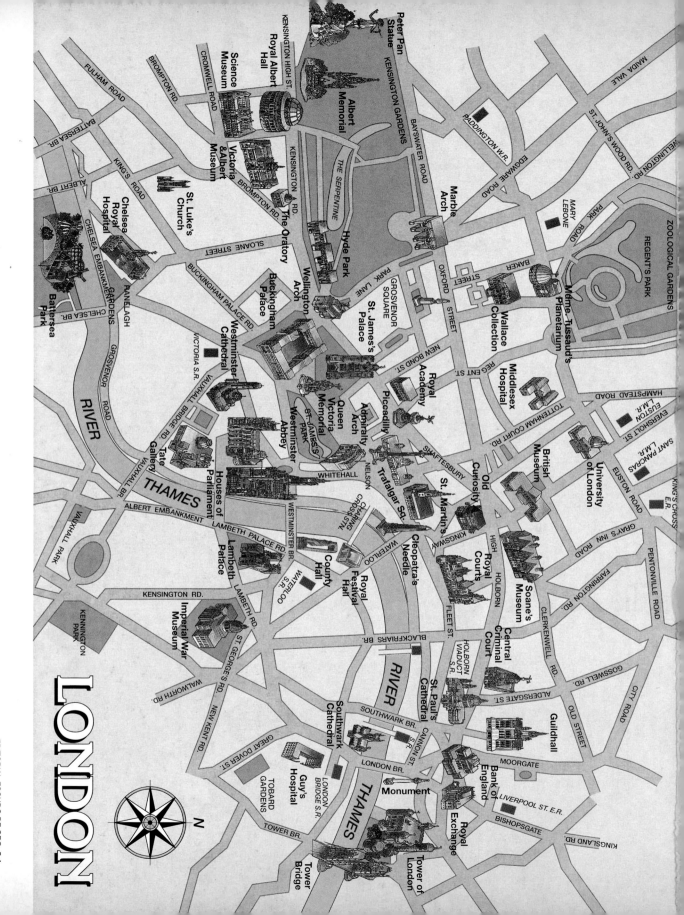

LONDON

EDITORIAL ESCUDO DE ORO, S.A.
I.S.B.N. 84-378-1010-8
Printed by FISA - Escudo de Oro, S.A.
Palaudàrias, 26 - 08004 Barcelona
Dep. Legal B. 4103-2004

Peter Pan Statue

Royal Albert Hall

Science Museum

Albert Memorial

KENSINGTON GARDENS

KENSINGTON HIGH ST.

BROMPTON RD.

CROMWELL ROAD

FULHAM ROAD

BATTERSEA BR.

ALBERT BR.

KING'S ROAD

Chelsea Royal Hospital

St. Luke's Church

Victoria & Albert Museum

The Oratory

KENSINGTON RD.

BROMPTON RD.

SLOANE STREET

SLOANE STREET

THE SERPENTINE

Hyde Park

Marble Arch

PADDINGTON W.R.

EDGWARE ROAD

MAIDA VALE

ST. JOHN'S WOOD RD.

WELLINGTON RD.

MARY LEBONE

PARK ROAD

BAKER STREET

REGENT'S PARK

ZOOLOGICAL GARDENS

Mme. Tussaud's Planetarium

Wallace Collection

OXFORD STREET

GROSVENOR SQUARE

PARK LANE

BAYSWATER ROAD

Battersea Park

CHELSEA EMBANKMENT GARDENS

RANELAGH GROSVENOR ROAD

BUCKINGHAM PALACE RD.

VICTORIA S.R.

VAUXHALL

Buckingham Palace

Westminster Cathedral

Wellington Arch

St. James's Palace

Queen Victoria Memorial

Westminster Abbey

ST. JAMES'S PARK

Admiralty Arch

WHITEHALL

NELSON

Trafalgar Sq.

St. Martin's

Piccadilly

Royal Academy

NEW BOND ST.

REGENT ST.

Middlesex Hospital

TOTTENHAM COURT RD.

British Museum

University of London

EUSTON L.M.R.

EVERSHOLT ST.

SAINT PANCRAS L.M.R.

EUSTON RD.

KING'S CROSS E.R.

HAMPSTEAD ROAD

GRAY'S INN ROAD

PENTONVILLE ROAD

FARRINGDON RD.

CLERKENWELL RD.

GOSSWELL RD.

OLD STREET

CITY ROAD

KINGSLAND RD.

Old Curiosity

Royal Courts

Soane's Museum

Central Criminal Court

HIGH HOLBORN

HOLBORN

FLEET ST.

HOLBORN VIADUCT S.R.

ALDERSGATE ST.

MOORGATE

Guildhall

Bank of England

Royal Exchange

LIVERPOOL ST. E.R.

BISHOPSGATE

Tower of London

Tower Br.

THAMES

Monument

LONDON BR.

LONDON BRIDGE S.R.

CANNON ST.

CANNON ST. S.R.

St. Paul's Cathedral

BLACKFRIARS BR.

RIVER

SOUTHWARK BR.

Southwark Cathedral

Guy's Hospital

TOBARD GARDENS

GREAT DOVER ST.

NEW KENT RD.

WALWORTH RD.

ST. GEORGE'S RD.

Imperial War Museum

KENNINGTON PARK

KENNINGTON RD.

VAUXHALL PARK

VAUXHALL BR.

RIVER

THAMES

ALBERT EMBANKMENT

LAMBETH PALACE RD.

LAMBETH RD.

Lambeth Palace

County Hall

WATERLOO S.R.

WESTMINSTER BR.

Royal Festival Hall

WATERLOO

Cleopatra's Needle

CHARING CROSS STN.

KINGSWAY

SHAFTESBURY

Houses of Parliament

Tate Gallery

VAUXHALL BRIDGE RD.

N